The Good Cook's Book of
COOKING FOR TWO
Rhona Newman

CONTENTS

This edition published 1982
by Octopus Books Limited
59 Grosvenor Street
London W1

© Cathay Books 1980
ISBN 0 7064 1809 3

Printed in USA

INTRODUCTION

Whether you are cooking for one, two or a large family, it is important to serve appetizing meals. Too often there is little incentive to cook proper meals for one or two people and too much tendency to use convenience foods or settle for 'fast foods'.

This exciting new cookbook is specially designed to provide nutritious, attractive dishes for two, with quantities carefully chosen to avoid waste. There are recipes suitable for all occasions, from quick snack lunches to intimate dinner parties for two.

Certain dishes, including Turkey fricassée, Crispy sage lamb and Orange pasta salad, are based on cooked ingredients, making excellent use of leftovers.

Most of the recipes are quick and easy to make, others may require a little planning. Whatever the occasion this practical cookbook will provide a source of inspiration when cooking for two.

NOTES

Standard spoon and cup measurements are used in all recipes.
All spoon and dry cup measures are level.

Fresh herbs are used unless otherwise stated. If unobtainable substitute a bouquet garni of the equivalent dried herbs, or use dried herbs instead but halve the quantities stated.

Use freshly ground black pepper where pepper is specified.

Ovens should be preheated to the specified temperature.

All recipes serve 2 unless otherwise stated.

BREAKFASTS

Tangy Grapefruit

1 grapefruit, halved
2-3 tablespoons
  raisins
¼ cup plain yogurt
1-2 tablespoons
  brown sugar
  (optional)

Cut the segments from each grapefruit half, discarding the pith and membranes and reserving the shells. Place the segments in a bowl and stir in the raisins and yogurt.

Spoon the mixture into the grapefruit shells and sprinkle with the sugar, if used. Refrigerate until serving time.

Bananas with Yogurt

2 bananas, sliced
1 cup vanilla yogurt
2 tablespoons
  chopped hazelnuts
2 tablespoons wheat
  germ

Divide the bananas between two bowls. Spoon the yogurt over the bananas and sprinkle with the hazelnuts and wheat germ.

Muesli

½ cup plain granola
¼ cup grapenuts
2 tablespoons raisins
1 tablespoon brown
  sugar
2 tablespoons toasted
  almonds
milk to serve

Place the granola, grapenuts, raisins, sugar and nuts in a bowl. Mix well and divide between two cereal bowls. Add milk just before serving.

Cereal Medley

2 zwieback, crushed
1 cup cornflakes
3 tablespoons bran
  cereal
1 apple, peeled,
  cored and grated
2 teaspoons brown
  sugar
2 tablespoons fruit
  yogurt
milk to serve

Place all the ingredients except the yogurt and milk in a bowl. Mix well and divide between two cereal bowls. Spoon the yogurt over and serve with milk.

9

Milk and Orange Egg Nog

1½ cups chilled milk
1 egg
2 tablespoons lemon
    yogurt
grated rind and juice
    of 1 orange
1 teaspoon honey
grated nutmeg

Beat the milk and egg together, then add the yogurt, orange rind and juice and honey. Continue beating until well blended.

Pour into drinking glasses and sprinkle with nutmeg to taste.

Kipper Toast

1 can (3¼ oz)
    kipper snacks
1 tablespoon butter or
    margarine
grated rind and juice
    of 1 lemon
1 tablespoon chopped
    parsley
pepper
2 slices wholewheat
    bread, toasted
parsley sprigs for
    garnish

Place the kippers in a small shallow flameproof dish, dot with butter and broil until hot and bubbly.

Place the fish in a bowl and mash with a fork. Add the lemon rind and juice, parsley and pepper to taste. Mix well, then spread the mixture over the toast slices.

Cook under a preheated broiler for 3 to 4 minutes. Garnish with parsley sprigs and serve immediately.

Beany Breakfast

1 can (8 oz) pork
    and beans
1 hard-cooked egg,
    chopped
½ cup chopped
    cooked ham
1 teaspoon
    Worcestershire
    sauce
1 teaspoon prepared
    mustard
1 tablespoon ketchup
salt and pepper
2 slices bread, toasted
1 tablespoon butter or
    margarine

Place the beans in a saucepan with the egg, ham, Worcestershire sauce, mustard and ketchup. Heat gently and add salt and pepper to taste.

Spread the toast with the butter and spoon the bean mixture on top. Serve immediately.

Onion and Tomato Scramble

3 eggs
2 tablespoons half
  and half
salt and pepper
2 tablespoons butter
  or margarine
1/2 small onion,
  finely chopped
1 tomato, peeled and
  chopped
2 slices bread, toasted

Beat the eggs with the half and half
and salt and pepper to taste.

Melt half the butter in a small
skillet, add the onion and sauté until
soft. Pour in the egg mixture and
cook slowly over low heat, stirring
until scrambled. Stir in the tomato
and remove from the heat.

Spread the toast with the
remaining butter and spoon the
scrambled egg mixture on top. Serve
immediately.

Cheese Topped Muffins

1 tablespoon butter or margarine
1 cup grated Cheddar cheese
½ teaspoon Dijon-style mustard
1 teaspoon milk
salt and pepper
2 English muffins
1 tomato, peeled and sliced
parsley sprigs for garnish

Melt the butter in a saucepan and add the cheese. Cook over low heat, stirring, until the cheese has melted. Stir in the mustard, milk and salt and pepper to taste.

Slice the English muffins in half and toast. Spread with the cheese mixture and top with the tomato slices. Cook under a preheated broiler for 2 to 3 minutes. Garnish with parsley. Serve immediately.

Sausage Parcels

4 breakfast sausages
prepared hot mustard
4 thin strips Cheddar cheese
2 slices bacon, halved

Cook the sausages under a preheated broiler for 6 to 8 minutes, turning to brown evenly. Spread with mustard to taste.

Place a strip of cheese on each sausage, then wrap a piece of bacon around. Return to the broiler for 6 to 8 minutes longer, turning once.

Serve with broiled tomatoes or baked beans.

FISH

Mackerel with Pineapple

2 mackerel, filleted
2 tablespoons
   all-purpose flour
salt and pepper
2 tablespoons butter
   or margarine
SAUCE:
½ cup canned
   crushed pineapple,
   drained
1 tablespoon lemon
   juice
pinch of grated
   nutmeg

Rinse and dry the mackerel fillets. Season the flour with salt and pepper to taste and sprinkle over the mackerel. Dot with butter and cook under a preheated broiler for 15 to 20 minutes.

To make the sauce, put all the ingredients into a saucepan. Cover and simmer until heated through.

Cool slightly, then process in a blender or food processor until smooth.

Place the mackerel on a warmed serving dish. Pour the sauce over. Serve immediately.

Haddock with Sour Cream and Mushrooms

¾ lb haddock fillet
salt and pepper
2 tablespoons butter
  or margarine
¼ cup water
SAUCE:
1 tablespoon butter or
  margarine
½ cup sliced
  mushrooms
½ cup sour cream
¼ teaspoon paprika
FOR GARNISH:
chopped parsley

Place the haddock in a small shallow baking dish. Sprinkle with salt and pepper, dot with the butter and add the water. Cover with foil and bake in a preheated 325°F oven for 20 minutes.

Meanwhile, make the sauce. Melt the butter in a saucepan, add the mushrooms and sauté for 1 minute. Stir in the sour cream, paprika and salt and pepper to taste. Heat through gently.

Drain the fish and transfer to a warmed serving dish. Pour the sauce over and garnish with chopped parsley. Serve immediately.

Cod with Lemon and Watercress Sauce

2 cod steaks
1 small onion, sliced
1 bay leaf
4 black peppercorns
grated rind of
   ½ lemon
3 tablespoons apple
   cider
salt and pepper
SAUCE:
2 teaspoons
   cornstarch
1 teaspoon lemon
   juice
1 egg yolk
¼ cup milk
½ bunch watercress,
   stems removed
FOR GARNISH:
watercress sprigs

Place the cod in a shallow baking dish. Add the onion, bay leaf, peppercorns, lemon rind, apple cider and salt to taste. Cover with foil and bake in a preheated 325°F oven for 20 minutes.

Transfer the fish to a warmed serving dish and remove the skin and bones. Keep hot. Strain the fish liquid and add enough water to make 5 tablespoons. Blend the cornstarch with the fish liquid and lemon juice. Heat, stirring, until thickened. Beat the egg yolk and milk together, then add to the sauce.

Finely chop the watercress. Add to the sauce with salt and pepper to taste. Heat gently but do not boil.

Pour the sauce over the fish. Serve immediately, garnished with watercress.

Sole with Banana and Nuts

¾ lb sole fillets
1 tablespoon butter or
   margarine
1 banana, sliced
¼ cup unsalted
   peanuts
¼ cup grated
   Cheddar cheese
SAUCE:
1 tablespoon butter or
   margarine
2 tablespoons
   all-purpose flour
⅔ cup milk
2 tablespoons plain
   yogurt
salt and pepper
FOR GARNISH:
parsley sprigs

Place the fish in a greased shallow baking dish. Dot with the butter and bake in a preheated 350°F oven for 10 minutes. Remove from the oven and arrange the banana and peanuts over the fish.

To make the sauce, melt the butter in a saucepan and stir in the flour. Cook for 1 minute, then gradually stir in the milk. Cook, stirring, until the sauce thickens. Stir in the yogurt and salt and pepper to taste.

Pour the sauce over the fish, sprinkle with the cheese and return to the oven. Bake for 15 minutes longer.

Garnish with parsley. Serve immediately.

Herb Fish Cakes

2 medium-size
  potatoes, chopped
1 small onion, sliced
salt and pepper
2 tablespoons milk
1 tablespoon butter or
  margarine
½ lb white fish
  fillet, chopped
2 teaspoons chopped
  parsley
½ teaspoon dried
  Italian seasoning
1 egg, separated
dry bread crumbs for
  coating
oil for frying
parsley sprigs for
  garnish

Cook the potatoes and onion in boiling salted water until soft. Drain and mash, then beat in the milk.

Melt the butter in a skillet, add the fish and fry for 10 to 12 minutes. Flake the fish and add to the potato. Stir in the herbs, egg yolk and salt and pepper to taste. Mix well, then let cool.

On a floured surface, divide the mixture into four and shape each piece into a flat cake. Lightly beat the egg white. Dip the fish cakes into the egg white, then coat with bread crumbs.

Heat the oil in a skillet and sauté the fish cakes until crisp and golden on both sides. Transfer to a warmed serving dish and garnish with parsley.

17

Tuna Vol-au-Vent

1 sheet (½ of a
    17¼ oz pkg)
    frozen puff pastry,
    thawed
1½ tablespoons butter
    or margarine
1 small onion,
    chopped
1½ tablespoons
    all-purpose flour
¾ cup milk
½ teaspoon Dijon-
    style mustard
½ cup grated Swiss
    cheese
1 can (7 oz) tuna
    fish, drained and
    flaked
1 tablespoon chopped
    parsley
salt and pepper

Roll out the pastry dough to a 7 inch
round. Score a round in the center
using a 3½ inch cookie cutter,
cutting halfway through the dough.

Place the round on a cookie sheet
and bake in a preheated 425°F oven
for 15 to 18 minutes or until risen
and golden brown.

Meanwhile, melt the butter in a
saucepan. Add the onion and sauté
until softened. Stir in the flour and
cook for 1 minute. Gradually stir in
the milk. Cook, stirring, until
thickened. Remove the saucepan
from the heat, add the mustard and
cheese and stir until the cheese has
melted. Add the tuna, parsley and
salt and pepper to taste and stir well.

Carefully remove the lid from the
vol-au-vent and set aside. Discard
any soft pastry in the center, making
a deep well. Fill the well with the
tuna mixture and replace the lid.
Serve immediately.

Crispy Tangy Fish

1 tablespoon butter or
  margarine
2 tablespoons
  all-purpose flour
¾ cup milk
1 tablespoon
  mayonnaise (see
  page 73)
½ teaspoon lemon
  juice
salt and pepper
½ lb white fish fillet
⅓ cup dry bread
  crumbs
4 slices bacon, cooked
  and crumbled
¼ cup grated
  Cheddar cheese
FOR GARNISH:
tomato slices

Melt the butter in a saucepan, stir in
the flour and cook for 1 minute.
Gradually stir in the milk and cook,
stirring, until the sauce thickens. Stir
in the mayonnaise, lemon juice and
salt and pepper to taste.

Place the fish in a shallow baking
dish and pour the sauce over.
Combine the bread crumbs, bacon
and cheese and sprinkle over the
sauce.

Bake in a preheated 375°F oven for
20 minutes, then place under the
broiler for 2 to 3 minutes to brown
the top.

Garnish with tomato slices. Serve
immediately.

Sardine and Egg Supper

1 can (8 oz) sardines
   in tomato sauce
1 hard-cooked egg,
   quartered
1 stalk celery, chopped
1/2 cup frozen peas,
   thawed
1/4 cup milk
   (approximately)
1 tablespoon butter or
   margarine
2 tablespoons
   all-purpose flour
pinch of sugar
salt and pepper
1/2 cup crushed potato
   chips
chopped parsley for
   garnish

Drain the sardines, reserving the sauce. Arrange the sardines in a shallow baking dish. Add the egg quarters to the dish. Scatter the celery and peas over the top.

Combine the reserved tomato sauce with enough milk to make 1 cup.

Melt the butter in a saucepan and stir in the flour. Cook for 1 minute, then gradually stir in the liquid. Cook, stirring, until the sauce thickens. Add the sugar and salt and pepper to taste.

Pour the sauce over the fish, sprinkle with the potato chips and bake in a preheated 350°F oven for 30 minutes. Garnish with parsley. Serve immediately.

Stuffed Haddock Parcels

2 tablespoons
  herb-seasoned dry
  stuffing mix
¼ cup boiling water
¼ cup grated
  Cheddar cheese
salt and pepper
2 haddock steaks
1 tablespoon butter or
  margarine
SAUCE:
1 tablespoon
  mayonnaise (see
  page 73)
1 tablespoon plain
  yogurt
1 teaspoon finely
  chopped parsley
¼ teaspoon dried
  thyme
FOR GARNISH:
watercress sprigs

Place the stuffing mix in a bowl and add the boiling water. Stir in the cheese and salt and pepper to taste.

Place each haddock steak on a piece of foil and spread with the stuffing. Dot with the butter and fold over the foil, enclosing the filling, to make parcels.

Place the parcels on a cookie sheet and bake in a preheated 375°F oven for 20 to 25 minutes. Fold back the foil and continue to bake for 5 to 10 minutes or until the topping is golden.

Blend all the sauce ingredients together, with salt and pepper to taste. Transfer the fish to a warmed serving dish. Garnish with watercress and serve the sauce separately.

21

Potato Cod Bake

¾ lb cod fillet
½ small onion,
   finely chopped
3 black peppercorns
1 small apple,
   peeled, cored and
   sliced
¼ teaspoon dried
   thyme
¼ cup apple cider
salt and pepper
4-5 tablespoons milk
1 tablespoon butter
2 tablespoons
   all-purpose flour
TOPPING:
1½ cups water
½ cup milk
2 tablespoons butter
   or margarine
grated nutmeg
salt and pepper
1 pkg (3¼ oz)
   instant mashed
   potato flakes

Place the cod, onion, peppercorns, apple, thyme, cider and salt to taste in a buttered baking dish. Cover and bake in a preheated 325°F oven for 20 minutes.

Strain the fish cooking liquid and make up to ¾ cup with the milk. Melt the butter in a saucepan and stir in the flour. Cook for 1 minute, then gradually stir in the fish liquid. Cook, stirring, until the sauce thickens. Add salt and pepper to taste.

Flake the fish and add to the sauce with the onion and apple. Heat through gently, then pour into the baking dish.

Bring the water, milk, butter and nutmeg, salt and pepper to taste to a boil. Remove from the heat and stir in the potato flakes.

Spread the potatoes over the fish and score a pattern on top with a fork. Place under a preheated broiler and brown for 2 to 3 minutes. Serve immediately.

Salmon Mousse

2 teaspoons
  unflavored gelatin,
  soaked in ⅔ cup
  water
⅔ cup light cream
2 eggs, separated
1 teaspoon lemon
  juice
½ teaspoon anchovy
  paste
salt and pepper
1 can (7¾ oz)
  salmon, drained
FOR GARNISH:
cucumber slices
parsley sprigs

Put the gelatin mixture in a bowl over a saucepan of gently simmering water and stir until dissolved. Cool slightly.

Warm the cream, then beat in the egg yolks. Add the gelatin mixture with the lemon juice, anchovy paste and salt and pepper to taste and mix well.

Remove any skin and bones from the salmon, then mash until smooth. Add to the egg mixture and mix until thoroughly blended.

Beat the egg whites until they form soft peaks. Fold into the salmon mixture. Spoon into a 3 cup (6 inch) soufflé dish and chill until set.

Serve garnished with cucumber and parsley.

Tuna Pasta Salad

1½-2 cups pasta
  shells
salt and pepper
½ cup sliced
  mushrooms
½ green pepper,
  seeded and chopped
1 can (8 oz)
  tomatoes, drained
  and chopped
1 can (3½ oz) tuna
  fish, drained and
  flaked
3 tablespoons oil
1 tablespoon lemon
  juice
garlic powder
chopped parsley for
  garnish

Cook the pasta in plenty of boiling salted water until *al dente* (tender but still firm to the bite). Drain and rinse thoroughly under cold running water.

Place the pasta in a serving bowl and add the mushrooms, green pepper, tomatoes and tuna.

Blend the oil with the lemon juice, then add garlic powder and pepper to taste. Pour the dressing over the pasta mixture and toss well.

Garnish with parsley before serving.

NOTE: The flavor improves if this dish is prepared the day before and refrigerated overnight.

Lamb in Red Currant and Mint Sauce

2 lamb chops
salt and pepper
*2 tablespoons butter
  or margarine*
1 small onion, sliced
*2 tablespoons
  all-purpose flour*
3/4 cup stock or broth
*2 teaspoons red
  currant jelly*
*1 teaspoon mint
  sauce*
pinch of sugar
*1 tablespoon light
  cream (optional)*
*mint sprigs for
  garnish*

Trim the chops and sprinkle with salt and pepper. Melt half the butter in a skillet, add the chops and cook for 10 to 15 minutes on each side. Drain and transfer to a warmed serving dish. Keep hot.

Melt the remaining butter in the skillet, add the onion and sauté until soft. Stir in the flour and cook for 1 minute. Gradually stir in the stock and cook, stirring, until the sauce thickens.

Add the red currant jelly, mint sauce, sugar and salt and pepper to taste. Stir in the cream, if used. Pour the sauce over the chops and garnish with mint.

Serve with new potatoes and peas.

Lamb Hotpot

1 lb lamb for stew
2 potatoes, sliced
salt and pepper
1 onion, sliced
2 carrots, sliced
1 stalk celery,
  chopped
½ teaspoon dried
  thyme
1 cup stock or broth
1 tablespoon butter or
  margarine, melted

Trim excess fat from the lamb.

Cover the bottom of a 1 quart casserole with half the potatoes. Arrange the lamb on top and sprinkle liberally with salt and pepper.

Combine the onion, carrots, celery and thyme with salt and pepper to taste. Spread over the lamb. Pour the stock over. Arrange the remaining potatoes in overlapping circles on top and brush with the butter.

Cover and bake in a preheated 350°F oven for 1½ hours. Remove the cover and continue to bake for 20 to 30 minutes or until the potatoes are browned.

Lamb Parcels

2 lamb chops
salt and pepper
1 tablespoon butter or
    margarine
1 sheet (½ of a
    17¼ oz pkg)
    frozen puff pastry,
    thawed
2 thin slices
    liverwurst
beaten egg to glaze
watercress sprigs for
    garnish

Sprinkle the chops with salt and pepper. Melt the butter in a skillet, add the chops and brown on both sides. Lower the heat and cook for 10 to 15 minutes. Drain on paper towels. Cool slightly.

Roll out the pastry dough to a rectangle about 12 × 6 inches, then cut in half to make two squares.

Spread the chops with the liverwurst, and place, liverwurst side down, on the dough squares. Brush the dough edges with water. Fold the dough over the chops and press the edges together to seal. Place on a cookie sheet, seam side down. Decorate with leaves cut from the dough trimmings. Brush with egg.

Bake in a preheated 425°F oven for 15 minutes. Lower the temperature to 350°F and bake for 15 to 20 minutes longer.

Transfer to a warmed serving dish and garnish with watercress.

Crispy Sage Lamb

1 tablespoon butter or
  margarine
½ onion, chopped
1 tablespoon
  all-purpose flour
¾ cup milk
1½ cups chopped
  cooked lamb
1 cup herb-seasoned
  dry stuffing mix
⅓ cup boiling water
½ teaspoon dried
  sage
¼ cup grated
  Cheddar cheese
salt and pepper
1 tomato, sliced, for
  garnish

Melt the butter in a saucepan, add
the onion and sauté until soft. Stir in
the flour, then gradually stir in the
milk. Cook, stirring, until the sauce
thickens. Add the lamb and heat
through.

Prepare the stuffing with the
boiling water as directed on the
package. Stir in the sage, cheese and
salt and pepper to taste.

Place the lamb in a greased
flameproof serving dish. Spoon the
stuffing over the top and place under
the broiler. Cook until the topping is
crisp and brown.

Garnish with the tomato slices.
Serve immediately.

Beef with Orange

1½ tablespoons
    all-purpose flour
salt and pepper
¾ lb chuck steak,
    cubed
1 tablespoon butter or
    margarine
1 small onion,
    chopped
½ green pepper,
    seeded and
    chopped
grated rind and juice
    of 1 orange
1 cup beef stock or
    broth
chopped parsley for
    garnish

Season the flour with salt and pepper and use to coat the meat. Melt the butter in a skillet, add the onion and green pepper and sauté until soft. Add the meat and cook, turning, until evenly browned. Transfer to a casserole.

Stir in the orange rind and juice, stock and salt and pepper to taste. Cover and bake in a preheated 325°F oven for 1 to 1¼ hours or until the meat is tender.

Serve hot, garnished with parsley.

Beef Crumble

½ lb lean ground
beef
1 small onion, finely
chopped
1 stalk celery, chopped
¼ cup chopped
mushrooms
1 small carrot, grated
1 teaspoon
all-purpose flour
⅔ cup beef stock or
broth
½ teaspoon Worcester-
shire sauce
salt and pepper
TOPPING:
¾ cup wholewheat
flour
3 tablespoons oatmeal
2 tablespoons butter
⅓ cup grated
Cheddar cheese
½ teaspoon dried
mixed herbs
FOR GARNISH:
parsley sprigs

Cook the beef in a skillet until it is brown and crumbly. Add the onion, celery, mushrooms and carrot and cook for 5 minutes. Stir in the flour and cook for 1 minute. Add the stock, Worcestershire sauce and salt and pepper to taste. Bring to a boil, stirring. Cover and simmer for 30 to 40 minutes.

To make the topping, place the flour and oatmeal in a bowl. Cut in the butter until the mixture resembles coarse bread crumbs. Stir in the cheese, herbs and salt and pepper to taste.

Transfer the meat mixture to a greased casserole and spoon the topping over. Bake in a preheated 375°F oven for 20 to 30 minutes.

Serve hot, garnished with parsley.

Chili Beef

1/4 cup dried red kidney beans
3/4 lb lean ground beef
1 onion, finely chopped
1/2 small green pepper, seeded and chopped
1 can (8 oz) tomatoes
2 tablespoons water
1 teaspoon chili powder
1/2 teaspoon cumin seeds
salt and pepper

Place the beans in a bowl and cover with cold water. Let soak overnight. Drain the beans, rinse and place in a saucepan. Cover with fresh cold water. Bring to a boil and boil for 10 minutes. Lower the heat and simmer for 25 minutes, then drain.

Cook the beef in a skillet until it is brown and crumbly. Add the onion and green pepper and sauté for 5 minutes. Stir in the tomatoes with their juice, the water, chili powder, cumin and salt and pepper to taste.

Bring to a boil, stirring, then add the beans. Cover and simmer for 1 hour.

Spoon into two warmed serving bowls. Serve hot, with a green salad and pitta bread, if desired.

Hamburgers with Barbecue Sauce

½ lb lean ground beef
2 teaspoons finely chopped onion
½ teaspoon prepared mustard
2 teaspoons chopped parsley
salt and pepper
1 tablespoon butter or margarine, melted
SAUCE:
1 tablespoon butter or margarine
1 onion, finely chopped
1 tablespoon ketchup
1 tablespoon vinegar
1 tablespoon brown sugar
pinch of chili powder
½ teaspoon dry mustard
½ teaspoon dried mixed herbs
6 tablespoons water

Place the ground beef, onion, mustard and parsley in a bowl. Add salt and pepper to taste and mix well. Divide the mixture into four and shape each piece into a hamburger.

To make the sauce, melt the butter in a small saucepan, add the onion and sauté until soft. Mix together the remaining sauce ingredients and add to the saucepan. Bring to a boil, cover and simmer for 20 minutes.

Brush the hamburgers with the melted butter and broil to desired degree of doneness, turning once.

Transfer to a warmed serving dish. Serve hot, with French fried potatoes and Frenchstyle green beans or peas. Pass the sauce separately.

Pork with Prunes

6 prunes
1 teaspoon lemon
    juice
1 tablespoon
    all-purpose flour
salt and pepper
2 boneless pork chops
1 tablespoon butter or
    margarine
1 teaspoon oil
⅔ cup apple cider
2 teaspoons red
    currant jelly
¼ cup heavy cream
chopped parsley for
    garnish

Place the prunes in a bowl and cover
with cold water. Add the lemon juice
and let soak overnight.

Season the flour with salt and
pepper and use to coat the meat.
Heat the butter and oil in a
flameproof casserole. Add the chops
and cook for 5 minutes on each side.
Add the cider, cover and simmer for
30 minutes or until the pork is tender.

Cook the prunes in the soaking
liquid for 20 minutes or until tender.

Transfer the meat and prunes to a
warmed serving dish with a slotted
spoon; keep hot. Add 3 tablespoons
of the prune liquid to the casserole.
Stir well and simmer until the sauce
is reduced and thickened.

Stir in the red currant jelly and
cream. Heat gently, then pour over
the pork. Garnish with parsley and
serve immediately.

Devonshire Pork Casserole

1 tablespoon
    shortening
1 small onion, sliced
1 clove garlic, crushed
¾ lb boneless pork
    cubes
2 teaspoons
    all-purpose flour
⅔ cup apple cider
3 tablespoons stock or
    broth
½ teaspoon dried
    sage
salt and pepper
1 apple, peeled,
    cored and sliced
2 tablespoons light
    cream
chopped parsley for
    garnish

Melt the shortening in a skillet, add
the onion and garlic and sauté until
soft. Add the pork and cook,
turning, until evenly browned.
Transfer the pork and onion to a
casserole with a slotted spoon.

Add the flour to the skillet and
cook for 1 minute. Gradually stir in
the cider and stock and cook,
stirring, until the sauce thickens.

Stir in the sage and salt and pepper
to taste. Arrange the apple slices in
the casserole and pour the sauce
over. Cover and bake in a preheated
350°F oven for 1½ hours.

Stir in the cream and transfer to a
warmed serving dish. Garnish with
parsley and serve immediately.

Pork with Orange and Apricots

1 tablespoon butter or
  margarine
2 pork chops
grated rind and juice
  of ½ orange
salt and pepper
1 small onion, finely
  chopped
½ green pepper,
  seeded and
  chopped
1 cup stock or broth
1 teaspoon cornstarch
pinch of sugar
⅓ cup dried apricots
watercress sprigs for
  garnish

Melt the butter in a skillet. Add the chops and cook on both sides until evenly browned.

Transfer to a shallow baking dish with a slotted spoon. Sprinkle with the orange rind and salt and pepper to taste.

Add the onion and green pepper to the skillet and sauté until soft. Stir in the stock. Blend the cornstarch with the orange juice and add to the skillet. Heat, stirring, until the sauce thickens. Add the sugar and salt and pepper to taste.

Arrange the apricots on top of the pork and pour the sauce over. Cover with foil and bake in a preheated 350°F oven for 1 to 1¼ hours.

Garnish with watercress before serving.

Honey and Apricot Ham

4-6 dried apricots
½ teaspoon prepared
  mustard
1 teaspoon honey
salt and pepper
2 ham steaks
2 teaspoons
  cornstarch
1 chicken bouillon
  cube, crumbled
parsley sprigs for
  garnish

Place the apricots in a bowl and cover with cold water. Let soak for 2 to 3 hours.

Combine the mustard, honey and pepper to taste. Spread this mixture over both sides of the ham steaks. Broil for 6 to 8 minutes on each side.

Drain the apricots, reserving the liquid; add enough water, if necessary, to make ⅔ cup. Blend the cornstarch with a little of the liquid, then stir in the remaining liquid.

Pour into a saucepan and cook, stirring, until the sauce thickens. Add the bouillon cube and apricots and simmer for 1 minute. Check the seasoning.

Place the ham steaks on a warmed serving dish and pour the sauce over. Garnish with parsley. Serve immediately.

Sausage and Blackeye Pea Casserole

1/4 cup dried blackeye
   peas
6 large pork sausages
1 small onion, finely
   chopped
1 can (8 oz)
   tomatoes
1/4 cup water
1 beef bouillon cube,
   crumbled
1/2 teaspoon dried
   mixed herbs
salt and pepper

Place the blackeye peas in a bowl, cover with cold water and let soak overnight. Drain, rinse and place in a saucepan. Cover with fresh cold water, bring to a boil and simmer for 45 minutes or until tender. Drain thoroughly.

Broil the sausages, turning frequently, until evenly browned. Cool slightly, then cut into 1/2 inch pieces. Place in a casserole.

Add the blackeye peas, onion, tomatoes with their juice, water, bouillon cube, herbs and salt and pepper to taste to the casserole. Mix well.

Cover the casserole and bake in a preheated 350°F oven for 45 minutes.

Serve hot, with baked potatoes.

Italian Veal Casserole

1 tablespoon oil
¾ lb veal for stew
1 clove garlic,
  crushed
1 small onion, sliced
½ green pepper,
  seeded and
  chopped
1 tomato, peeled and
  chopped
1 cup stock or broth
salt and pepper
1 bouquet garni
chopped parsley for
  garnish

Heat the oil in a skillet, add the veal and sauté, turning, until golden brown all over. Add the garlic and onion and sauté until they are soft.

Stir in the green pepper, tomato, stock and salt and pepper to taste. Transfer to a casserole. Add the bouquet garni. Cover and bake in a preheated 350°F oven for 1 to 1½ hours.

Remove the bouquet garni and skim off any excess fat. Serve hot, garnished with parsley.

Veal Escalopes

2 veal cutlets
2 tablespoons butter
  or margarine
1 tablespoon oil
½ small onion, sliced
½ cup small
  mushrooms
2 tablespoons dry
  sherry
¼ cup heavy cream
salt and pepper
paprika
FOR GARNISH:
2 lemon twists
1 teaspoon chopped
  parsley

Snip the edges of the cutlets to
prevent the meat from curling up.

Heat the butter and oil in a skillet,
add the onion and sauté for 2 to 3
minutes. Add the veal and
mushrooms and cook for 8 to 10
minutes, turning the cutlets once,
until golden brown on both sides.

Stir in the sherry and bring to a
boil. Add the cream and heat
through, stirring. Add salt and
pepper to taste.

Lift the veal cutlets onto a warmed
serving dish and spoon the sauce
over. Sprinkle with paprika to taste.
Garnish each cutlet with a lemon
twist and chopped parsley.

Piquant Liver

4 slices bacon
1 tablespoon butter or
    margarine
1 small onion,
    chopped
2 tablespoons
    all-purpose flour
salt and pepper
2 slices beef or calves'
    liver
½ cup sliced
    mushrooms
⅔ cup stock or broth
1 tablespoon tomato
    paste
¼ teaspoon prepared
    mustard
2 teaspoons chutney
½ teaspoon sugar
chopped parsley for
    garnish

Cook the bacon until crisp. Drain on paper towels, crumble and reserve. Melt the butter in a skillet, add the onion and sauté until soft.

Season the flour with salt and pepper and use to coat the liver. Add to the skillet and cook, turning, until evenly browned. Stir in the bacon, mushrooms, stock, tomato paste, mustard, chutney and sugar. Add salt and pepper to taste. Bring to a boil, stirring, then cover and simmer for 20 minutes.

Transfer to a warmed serving dish and garnish with parsley. Serve immediately.

Sweetbreads in Sour Cream Sauce

1 pair sweetbreads
1 tablespoon vinegar
    or lemon juice or
    margarine
2 tablespoons butter
1 large onion, sliced
1 cup sliced
    mushrooms
1 cup sour cream
2 teaspoons prepared
    horseradish
1 tablespoon chopped
    dill
salt and pepper
toast points
FOR GARNISH:
paprika
watercress sprigs

Parboil the sweetbreads in water to which the vinegar has been added for 15 minutes. Drain well, then remove the outer membrane and thinly slice. Melt the butter in a skillet. Add the sliced sweetbreads and sauté until lightly browned. Remove with a slotted spoon and keep warm.

Add the onion and mushrooms to the skillet and sauté until the onion is soft. Stir in the sour cream, horseradish and dill. Return the sweetbreads to the skillet and cook until just heated through. Do not boil.

Spoon the sweetbreads over toast points, sprinkle with paprika and garnish with watercress sprigs. Serve immediately.

Sherried Chicken Livers

3 slices bacon
¼ cup all-purpose
  flour
salt and pepper
¾ lb chicken livers
1 small onion,
  chopped
1 clove garlic,
  crushed
1 cup beef stock or
  broth
1 tablespoon chopped
  parsley
½ cup sliced water
  chestnuts
¼ cup dry sherry

Cook the bacon in a skillet until crisp. Remove from the skillet, drain on paper towels and crumble.

Season the flour with salt and pepper and use to coat the chicken livers. Add the livers to the skillet and cook for about 7 minutes or until tender. Remove the chicken livers and keep warm.

Add the onion and garlic to the skillet and sauté until soft. Stir in the remaining seasoned flour and cook for 1 minute. Add the beef stock and parsley and cook, stirring, until thickened.

Return the chicken livers to the skillet with the water chestnuts. Stir in the sherry and cook until heated through. Sprinkle over the bacon and serve on a bed of hot cooked rice.

Curried Chicken

1 tablespoon butter or
  margarine
1 small onion, chopped
½ green pepper,
  seeded and chopped
1 tablespoon curry
  powder
2 tablespoons
  all-purpose flour
1¼ cups chicken
  stock or broth
1 small apple, cored
  and chopped
1 tablespoon shredded
  coconut
1 tablespoon sweet
  chutney
3 tablespoons golden
  raisins
salt and pepper
2 cups chopped
  cooked chicken
chopped parsley for
  garnish

Melt the butter in a saucepan, add
the onion and green pepper and sauté
until soft. Add the curry powder and
flour and continue cooking for 1
minute. Gradually stir in the stock
and cook, stirring, until thickened.

Stir in the apple, coconut, chutney,
raisins and salt and pepper to taste.
Cover and simmer for 10 minutes.
Add the chicken and continue
cooking for 20 minutes.

Sprinkle with parsley and serve
hot, with boiled rice.

Peanut and Cumin Chicken

2 tablespoons oil
1/2 broiler/fryer,
  halved
1 small onion, sliced
2 teaspoons
  all-purpose flour
2 teaspoons creamy
  peanut butter
2/3 cup chicken stock
  or broth
1/2 teaspoon cumin
  seeds
salt and pepper
1 tablespoon chopped
  peanuts for garnish

Heat the oil in a skillet, add the chicken pieces and sauté until brown on all sides. Drain and transfer to a casserole.

Sauté the onion in the oil remaining in the skillet until soft. Stir in the flour and peanut butter and cook for 1 minute. Gradually stir in the stock and bring to a boil. Add the cumin and season liberally with salt and pepper.

Pour the sauce over the chicken. Cover and bake in a preheated 350°F oven for 1 to 1 1/4 hours or until the chicken is tender.

Serve hot, sprinkled with chopped peanuts.

Maryland Chicken

2 tablespoons
   all-purpose flour
salt and pepper
4 chicken drumsticks
1 egg, beaten
3 tablespoons soft
   bread crumbs
1 tablespoon oil
2 tablespoons butter
   or margarine
ACCOMPANIMENTS:
4 slices bacon
2 bananas
1 tablespoon butter or
   margarine
1 can (8 oz) whole
   kernel corn
FOR GARNISH:
watercress sprigs

Season the flour with salt and pepper and use to coat the drumsticks. Dip into the egg, then coat with the bread crumbs.

Heat the oil and butter in a skillet, add the chicken and sauté, turning, until golden brown all over. Lower the heat, cover and cook gently for 15 to 20 minutes, turning occasionally, until the chicken is tender.

Halve the bacon slices, roll up and thread onto a skewer. Broil for about 3 minutes.

Cut the bananas in half lengthwise. Melt the butter in a saucepan, add the bananas and cook gently until golden. Heat the corn in a saucepan, then drain thoroughly.

Drain the chicken and transfer to a warmed serving platter. Arrange the corn around the chicken and place the bananas and bacon rolls on top.

Garnish with watercress and serve immediately.

Tangy Chicken Salad

3 tablespoons raisins
2 cups chopped
   cooked chicken
1/2 cup chopped celery
1/2 bunch watercress,
   chopped
juice of 1/2 orange
2/3 cup mayonnaise
   (see page 73)
salt and pepper
FOR GARNISH:
watercress sprigs
orange segments

Place the raisins in a bowl and cover with warm water. Let soak for 2 hours, then drain.

Put the chicken in a bowl with the celery, watercress and raisins.

Mix the orange juice with the mayonnaise and add salt and pepper to taste. Add to the chicken and mix well.

Spoon onto a serving dish and garnish with watercress and orange segments. Serve cold with rice and a green salad.

42

Chicken and Bacon Pie

1 tablespoon butter or
  margarine
1 small onion,
  chopped
½ apple, peeled,
  cored and chopped
2 tablespoons
  all-purpose flour
¾ cup chicken stock
  or broth
½ teaspoon dried
  thyme
1¼ cups chopped
  cooked chicken
4 slices bacon, cooked
  and crumbled
salt and pepper
PASTRY:
1 cup all-purpose
  flour
pinch of salt
2 tablespoons butter
  or margarine
2 tablespoons
  shortening
3 tablespoons cold
  water
beaten egg to glaze

Melt the butter in a saucepan, add
the onion and apple and sauté until
soft. Stir in the flour and cook for
1 minute. Gradually stir in the stock
and cook, stirring, until thickened.
Add the thyme, chicken, bacon and
salt and pepper to taste. Transfer to a
shallow casserole.

To make the pastry, sift the flour
and salt into a bowl. Cut in the
butter and shortening until the
mixture resembles fine bread
crumbs. Add the water and mix to a
firm dough. Knead lightly, then chill
for 15 minutes.

Roll out on a floured surface to a
round 1½ inches larger in diameter
than the casserole. Cut a 1 inch strip
from the edge of the round and place
on the dampened rim of the
casserole. Brush with water and
place the dough round in position,
making a hole in the center. Seal,
trim and flute the edges. Decorate
with leaves made from the dough
trimmings.

Brush with egg and bake in a
preheated 400°F oven for 20 to
30 minutes. Serve hot.

43

Apple and Cherry Duckling

2 tablespoons butter
    or margarine
1 small duckling,
    cut up
1 small onion, chopped
2 teaspoons
    all-purpose flour
²/₃ cup stock or broth
2 tablespoons dry
    vermouth
    (optional)
1 tablespoon red
    currant jelly
½ teaspoon sugar
salt and pepper
1 apple, peeled,
    cored and chopped
½ cup pitted dark
    sweet cherries

Melt the butter in a large skillet, add the duckling and cook, turning, until evenly browned. Transfer to a casserole with a slotted spoon.

Sauté the onion in the skillet until soft. Stir in the flour and cook for 1 minute. Gradually stir in the stock and vermouth, if used. Cook, stirring until thickened. Add the red currant jelly and sugar. Season liberally with salt and pepper.

Arrange the apple and cherries on top of the duckling and pour the sauce over. Cook and bake in a preheated 350°F oven for 1¼ to 1½ hours. Serve hot.

Turkey Fricassée

1 small onion,
  chopped
1 small carrot, grated
1 stalk celery,
  chopped
²⁄₃ cup stock or broth
1 bouquet garni
salt and pepper
²⁄₃ cup milk
  (approximately)
1 tablespoon butter or
  margarine
2 tablespoons
  all-purpose flour
grated nutmeg
2 cups chopped
  cooked turkey
1 tablespoon light
  cream
chopped parsley for
  garnish

Place the onion, carrot, celery, stock
and bouquet garni in a saucepan.
Add salt and pepper to taste. Bring
to a boil, cover and simmer for
15 minutes.

Strain the stock into a measuring
cup, reserving the vegetables, and
add enough milk to make 1¼ cups.

Melt the butter in a separate
saucepan, stir in the flour and cook
for 1 minute. Gradually stir in the
liquid and cook, stirring, until
thickened. Add nutmeg, salt and
pepper to taste.

Stir in the vegetables and turkey.
Cover and simmer for 15 minutes.
Remove from the heat and stir in the
cream.

Transfer to a warmed serving dish
and sprinkle with parsley. Serve
immediately.

EGG & CHEESE DISHES

Crispy Tuna and Egg

1 can (3½ oz) tuna
   fish, drained and
   flaked
¼ cup frozen whole
   kernel corn
2 hard-cooked eggs,
   chopped
1 tablespoon butter or
   margarine
2 tablespoons
   all-purpose flour
¾ cup milk
½ cup grated
   Cheddar cheese
2 teaspoons chopped
   chives
salt and pepper
½ cup crushed potato
   chips
chopped chives
   for garnish

Place the tuna in a shallow baking
dish. Spoon the corn and eggs on the
top.

Melt the butter in a saucepan, stir
in the flour and cook for 1 minute.
Gradually stir in the milk and cook,
stirring, until the sauce thickens.
Add the cheese, chives and salt and
pepper to taste. Pour the sauce over
the fish.

Sprinkle with the potato chips and
bake in a preheated 350°F oven for
30 minutes.

Serve hot, garnished with chives.

Farmhouse Omelet

1 tablespoon butter or
  margarine
1 onion, chopped
1 potato, diced
2 slices bacon,
  chopped
¼ cup chopped
  mushrooms
3 eggs
2 tablespoons milk
¼ teaspoon dried
  mixed herbs
salt and pepper
½ cup grated
  Cheddar cheese
chopped parsley for
  garnish

Melt the butter in a skillet, add the onion, potato and bacon and cook gently until soft. Add the mushrooms, increase the heat and cook until the vegetables begin to brown.

Beat the eggs, milk and herbs with salt and pepper to taste. Pour over the vegetables, tilting the skillet to spread the mixture evenly. Cook over moderate heat until the omelet starts to set.

Sprinkle with the cheese and place the skillet under a preheated broiler, keeping the oven door slightly ajar. Cook until the cheese is bubbling and golden brown.

Sprinkle with parsley and cut the omelet in half. Remove to warmed serving plates and serve immediately.

Creamy Onion Quiche

PASTRY:
1 cup all-purpose
  flour
pinch of salt
2 tablespoons butter
  or margarine
2 tablespoons
  shortening
3 tablespoons cold
  water
FILLING:
1 tablespoon butter or
  margarine
2 onions, thinly
  sliced
2 eggs
1/2 cup light cream
salt and pepper
FOR GARNISH:
chopped chives

Prepare and chill the dough as for
Chicken and Bacon Pie (see page 43).
Roll out and use to line a 7 inch
quiche or flan dish.

For the filling, melt the butter in a
skillet, add the onions and sauté until
soft. Spoon into the pastry shell.
Beat the eggs and cream with salt
and pepper to taste. Pour the egg
mixture over the onions.

Bake in a preheated 400°F oven for
25 to 35 minutes or until the filling is
set.

Serve hot or cold, garnished with
chives.

2 to 3 servings

Bean and Egg Curry

1/4 cup dried navy
  beans
1 tablespoon butter or
  margarine
1 onion, chopped
1 stalk celery,
  chopped
1 teaspoon curry
  powder
1/4 teaspoon ground
  ginger
1 tablespoon
  all-purpose flour
2/3 cup stock or broth
1 can (8 oz)
  tomatoes
salt and pepper
4 hard-cooked eggs
chopped parsley for
  garnish

Place the beans in a bowl, cover with
cold water and let soak overnight.

Drain, rinse and place in a
saucepan. Cover with fresh cold
water, bring to a boil and simmer for
45 minutes or until tender, then
drain.

Melt the butter in a saucepan, add
the onion and celery and sauté until
soft. Add the curry powder, ginger
and flour and continue to cook for
1 minute. Gradually stir in the stock
and tomatoes with their juice. Cook,
stirring, until thickened. Add the
beans and salt and pepper to taste.
Simmer for 15 minutes.

Cut the eggs in half lengthwise
and add to the curry. Cover and
cook until heated through. Transfer
to a warmed serving dish and garnish
with parsley. Serve immediately.

Savory Cheese Bake

2 slices bread
1 tablespoon butter or
   margarine
2 slices cooked ham,
   chopped
2 tablespoons cooked
   peas
1 egg, beaten
²/₃ cup milk
½ teaspoon prepared
   mustard
salt and pepper
½ cup grated
   Cheddar cheese
tomato slices for
   garnish

Spread the bread with the butter and
cut into triangles. Arrange in the
bottom of a casserole. Top with the
ham and peas.

Beat together the egg, milk,
mustard and salt and pepper to taste.
Pour into the dish and sprinkle the
cheese on top. Bake in a preheated
375°F oven for 20 to 25 minutes or
until golden and risen.

Garnish with tomato slices. Serve
immediately.

Cheese Fondue

1 clove garlic, halved
1 tablespoon butter or
  margarine
6 tablespoons dry
  white wine
1 cup grated Cheddar
  cheese
1 cup grated Swiss
  cheese
1 teaspoon cornstarch
1 tablespoon brandy
pepper
grated nutmeg
cubes of crusty bread

Rub the inside of a fondue pot, flameproof casserole or saucepan with the cut garlic clove. Add the butter and wine and heat gently. Add the cheeses and cook gently, stirring, until melted.

Blend the cornstarch and brandy to a smooth paste. Add pepper and nutmeg to taste and stir into the fondue. Continue to cook for 3 to 4 minutes or until smooth and creamy.

To serve, keep the fondue warm at the table, preferably over an alcohol burner. Place the bread on a serving plate. Each person then spears a piece of bread onto a long-handled fondue fork and dips it into the fondue. Serve with a green salad.

Scone Pizzas

1 cup self-rising flour
pinch of dry mustard
salt and pepper
2 tablespoons butter
  or margarine
6 tablespoons milk
TOPPING:
1 can (16 oz)
  tomatoes, drained
  and chopped
2 teaspoons grated
  onion
1/4 teaspoon dried
  oregano
1/4 teaspoon dried
  basil
2 slices salami,
  chopped
1 cup grated
  Mozzarella cheese
6 stuffed olives,
  sliced

Sift the flour with the mustard and salt and pepper to taste into a bowl. Cut in the butter until the mixture resembles fine bread crumbs. Stir in the milk and mix to a firm dough. Place on a floured surface and knead until smooth.

Divide the dough in half. Roll out each piece to a 6 to 7 inch round and place on a large greased cookie sheet.

Arrange the tomatoes on top and sprinkle with the onion, herbs and salt and pepper to taste. Sprinkle the salami and Mozzarella cheese over the pizza and top with the olives.

Bake in a preheated 400°F oven for 15 to 20 minutes or until the cheese is brown and bubbling. Serve warm, with a mixed salad.

Cheese-Topped Sandwiches

4 slices bacon, chopped
½ cup sliced
    mushrooms
2 tomatoes, peeled
    and chopped
½ teaspoon prepared
    mustard
salt and pepper
2 tablespoons butter
    or margarine
4 slices wholewheat
    bread
½ cup grated
    Cheddar cheese
parsley sprigs for
    garnish

Partially cook the bacon in a skillet. Add the mushrooms and tomatoes and cook for 1 minute. Stir in the mustard and salt and pepper to taste.

Butter the bread. Spread the bacon mixture on two of the bread slices and top with the remaining two slices. Toast both sides of the sandwiches under a preheated broiler until golden brown.

Sprinkle the cheese on top and return to the broiler. Broil until the cheese is golden and bubbling.

Garnish with parsley. Serve immediately.

Vegetarian Turnovers

PASTRY:
1 cup all-purpose
   flour
pinch of salt
2 tablespoons butter
   or margarine
2 tablespoons
   shortening
3 tablespoons cold
   water
FILLING:
¾ cup cooked mixed
   vegetables
2 tablespoons baked
   beans
½ cup diced Cheddar
   cheese
1 tablespoon chutney
1 egg yolk, beaten
salt and pepper
milk for glazing
FOR GARNISH:
parsley sprigs

Prepare and chill the dough as for
Chicken and Bacon Pie (see page 43).
Divide in half and roll out each piece
to a 6 inch round.

Mix together the vegetables,
beans, cheese, chutney, most of the
egg yolk and salt and pepper to taste.
Divide between the dough rounds,
leaving a ½ inch border at the edges.

Add a little milk to the remaining
egg yolk and use to brush the dough
edges. Fold the rounds in half,
enclosing the filling, and crimp the
edges together. Place on a cookie
sheet.

Make slits in the top and brush the
turnovers with the remaining egg
yolk mixture. Bake in a preheated
375°F oven for 20 to 25 minutes.

Serve hot or cold, garnished with
parsley.

Cottage Cheese and Spinach Quiche

PASTRY:
1 cup all-purpose
   flour
pinch of salt
2 tablespoons butter
   or margarine
2 tablespoons
   shortening
3 tablespoons cold
   water
FILLING:
½ pkg (10 oz)
   frozen chopped
   spinach, thawed
salt and pepper
½ cup small curd
   cottage cheese
1 egg, beaten
2 tablespoons sour cream
grated nutmeg
¼ cup grated Swiss
   cheese

Make and chill the dough as for
Chicken and Bacon Pie (see page 43).
Roll out and use to line a 7 inch
quiche or flan dish.

Drain the spinach and squeeze dry.
Scatter in the pastry shell. Sprinkle
with salt and pepper to taste.

Combine the cottage cheese, egg,
sour cream, and salt, pepper and
nutmeg to taste. Pour over the
spinach and sprinkle with the grated
cheese.

Bake in a preheated 400°F oven for
25 to 35 minutes or until the filling is
set. Serve hot or cold.
3 servings

Cheese Pots

1/3 cup crumbled
   Stilton cheese
2 tablespoons butter
   or margarine,
   softened
1/2 cup grated
   Cheddar cheese
2 tablespoons milk
1 clove garlic,
   crushed
1 teaspoon chopped
   chives
salt and pepper
parsley sprigs for
   garnish

Place the Stilton and butter in a bowl and beat with a wooden spoon until thoroughly blended. Beat in the Cheddar cheese and milk. Add the garlic, chives and salt and pepper to taste.

Divide the mixture between two small ramekins and chill before serving. Garnish with parsley and serve with toast.

Cheese Medley Coleslaw

1½ cups shredded
   cabbage
1 carrot, grated
1 stalk celery,
   chopped
¼ cup diced Edam
   cheese
¼ cup diced Cheddar
   cheese
¼ cup diced Stilton
   cheese
3 tablespoons plain
   yogurt
2 tablespoons
   mayonnaise (see
   page 73)
salt and pepper
chopped parsley for
   garnish

Place the vegetables and cheeses in a
serving bowl and mix.

Combine the yogurt and
mayonnaise with salt and pepper to
taste. Pour the dressing over the
salad and toss well.

Sprinkle with parsley. Serve with
crusty rolls and butter.

Stilton Cauliflower

1 small cauliflower,
   broken into florets
salt and pepper
1 tablespoon butter or
   margarine
2 tablespoons
   all-purpose flour
¾ cup milk
½ cup crumbled
   Stilton cheese
1 tablespoon dry
   bread crumbs

Cook the cauliflower in boiling salted water for about 12 minutes or until tender. Drain and transfer to a warmed flameproof serving dish.

Melt the butter in a saucepan, stir in the flour and cook for 1 minute. Gradually stir in the milk and cook, stirring, until thickened.

Stir in the cheese and heat gently, stirring, until melted. Add salt and pepper to taste.

Pour the sauce over the cauliflower and top with the bread crumbs. Cook under a preheated broiler until the top is golden brown. Serve hot.

Caraway Cabbage

3 cups shredded red
  or white cabbage
1 small onion, chopped
½ teaspoon caraway
  seeds
salt and pepper
1 tablespoon butter or
  margarine, melted
½ red pepper, seeded
  and sliced

Cook the cabbage, onion and
caraway seeds in boiling salted water
for 5 to 8 minutes or until just
tender. Drain and return to the pan.

Add the butter and red pepper and
toss the ingredients over low heat for
1 minute. Add salt and pepper to
taste and transfer to a warmed
serving dish. Serve immediately.

Vegetarian Hotpot

¼ cup dried chick
   peas
¼ cup dried navy
   beans
¼ cup dried blackeye
   peas
¼ cup dried red
   kidney beans
1 tablespoon butter or
   margarine
1 small onion,
   chopped
1 carrot, sliced
1 stalk celery,
   chopped
1 clove garlic,
   crushed
1 can (8 oz)
   tomatoes
½ teaspoon dried
   Italian seasoning
salt and pepper
½ cup grated
   Parmesan cheese

Place the chick peas, navy beans and
blackeye peas in a bowl and cover
with cold water. Place the kidney
beans in a separate bowl and cover
with water. Let soak overnight.

Drain and place the chick peas,
navy beans and blackeye peas in a
saucepan; put the kidney beans in a
separate pan (to avoid turning the
other beans pink). Cover the peas
and beans with fresh cold water.
Bring to a boil and boil for 10
minutes. Cover and simmer for
40 minutes or until tender. Drain,
rinse under cold water, then
thoroughly drain.

Melt the butter in a saucepan, add
until soft. Stir in the garlic, peas,
beans, tomatoes with their juice,
herbs and salt and pepper to taste.
salt and pepper to taste.

Bring to a boil, cover and simmer
for 1 to 1¼ hours, adding a little
water if the mixture becomes too
dry. Check the seasoning. Transfer
to a warmed serving dish. Sprinkle
with the cheese. Serve immediately.

Spiced Vegetables and Rice

½ cup brown rice
1¼ cups boiling water
salt and pepper
1 tablespoon oil
2 leeks, sliced
1 carrot, thinly sliced
1 onion, sliced
½ apple, cored and
  chopped
½ teaspoon cumin
  seeds
½ teaspoon ground
  coriander
pinch of cayenne
  pepper
4-5 tablespoons stock
chopped parsley for
  garnish

Cook the rice in the boiling salted water for 45 to 50 minutes or until tender.

Meanwhile, heat the oil in a saucepan, add the leeks, carrot, onion and apple and sauté, stirring, for 3 minutes. Add the cumin, coriander, cayenne and salt and pepper to taste. Continue to cook for 3 minutes, then stir in the stock. Cover and simmer for 10 to 15 minutes or until the vegetables are tender.

Stir the rice into the vegetables and cook gently for 5 minutes. Transfer to a warmed serving dish and garnish with parsley. Serve hot.

Mediterranean Vegetables

1 small eggplant
salt and pepper
1½ tablespoons oil
1 small onion, sliced
1 clove garlic, crushed
1 stalk celery,
  chopped
½ green pepper,
  seeded and chopped
2 tomatoes, peeled
  and chopped
2 tablespoons water
½ teaspoon dried
  oregano
½ teaspoon dried
  basil
chopped parsley for
  garnish

Cut the eggplant into thin slices and sprinkle with salt. Place in a colander and let stand for 30 minutes. Rinse and pat dry with paper towels.

Heat the oil in a skillet and add the eggplant, onion, garlic, celery and green pepper. Cook, stirring, until all the vegetables are coated with oil. Cover and cook for 10 minutes.

Add the tomatoes, water, oregano, basil and salt and pepper to taste. Bring to a boil, cover and simmer for 30 minutes.

Serve hot or cold, sprinkled with parsley.

Minted Zucchini with Peas and Corn

½ lb zucchini,
  thinly sliced
salt
½ cup frozen peas
½ cup frozen whole
  kernel corn
2 mint sprigs
1 tablespoon butter or
  margarine
2 teaspoons chopped
  chives

Place the zucchini in a saucepan of boiling salted water. Add the peas, corn and mint. Cover and simmer for 5 minutes or until the vegetables are just tender. Drain the vegetables well, remove the mint and return the vegetables to the saucepan.

Add the butter and chives and toss over low heat for 1 minute. Transfer to a warmed serving dish. Serve hot.

French-Style Peas

1 pkg (10 oz) frozen
    peas
3 lettuce leaves,
    shredded
2 tablespoons butter
3 scallions, finely
    chopped
1/2 teaspoon sugar
1/4 cup chicken stock
    or broth
1 sprig each parsley
    and mint, tied
    together.
salt and pepper

Place all the ingredients in a
saucepan, adding salt and pepper to
taste. Slowly bring to a boil, cover
and simmer for 10 to 12 minutes or
until the peas are tender, adding
more stock or water if necessary.

Discard the parsley and mint.
Transfer to a warmed serving dish.
Serve immediately.

Potatoes with Sour Cream

3 medium-size
   potatoes, thinly
   sliced
1 small onion, finely
   chopped
¼ cup sour cream
salt and pepper
3 tablespoons butter
   or margarine
⅓ cup milk
chopped chives for
   garnish

Place a layer of potatoes in the bottom of a greased shallow baking dish. Add a little of the onion and sour cream. Season with salt and pepper. Repeat the layers and finish with a layer of potatoes.

Melt 2 tablespoons of the butter in a saucepan, stir in the milk and pour over the potatoes. Dot with the remaining butter.

Cover and bake in a preheated 375°F oven for 45 minutes. Uncover and bake for 20 minutes longer or until the potatoes are tender and golden brown.

Garnish with chives. Serve hot with lamb chops or baked ham.

Baked Zucchini

1 tablespoon butter or
   margarine
1 small onion,
   chopped
1/2 lb zucchini, sliced
1 large tomato,
   peeled and sliced
1/2 teaspoon dried
   oregano
salt and pepper
1 egg, beaten
1/2 cup grated
   Gruyère cheese
parsley sprigs for
   garnish

Melt the butter in a saucepan, add the onion and zucchini and sauté for 2 minutes. Transfer to a shallow baking dish and place the tomato slices on top. Sprinkle with the oregano and salt and pepper to taste.

Combine the egg, cheese and salt and pepper to taste. Spoon over the tomatoes. Bake in a preheated 350°F oven for 15 to 20 minutes or until the top is golden.

Garnish with parsley. Serve hot.

Savory Stuffed Peppers

2 medium-size green
    peppers
salt and pepper
1 tablespoon butter or
    margarine
1/2 small onion,
    finely chopped
1 cup cooked rice
2 slices bacon, cooked
    and crumbled
1/2 cup grated
    Cheddar cheese
1/4 cup light cream
1/4 teaspoon prepared
    mustard
1 teaspoon chopped
    parsley
1 teaspoon chopped
    basil (optional)
grated nutmeg

Cut the tops from the peppers and reserve; discard the seeds and cores. Blanch the peppers in boiling salted water for 2 minutes. Drain.

Melt the butter in a saucepan, add the onion and sauté until soft. Remove from the heat and stir in the rice, bacon and cheese.

Beat the cream with the mustard, parsley, basil if used, and nutmeg, salt and pepper to taste, then stir into the rice mixture. Spoon into the pepper shells. Replace the tops.

Place in a shallow baking dish, cover with foil and bake in a preheated 350°F oven for 15 to 20 minutes. Serve hot.

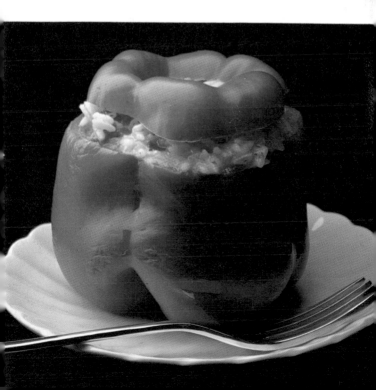

Bean Sprout Salad

¼ lb bean sprouts
1 stalk celery,
  chopped
1 carrot, grated
1 inch piece
  cucumber, cut into
  julienne strips
3 tablespoons raisins
2 tablespoons French
  dressing (see page
  73)
1 tablespoon plain
  yogurt
salt and pepper

Place the bean sprouts, celery, carrot, cucumber and raisins in a bowl.

Combine the French dressing with the yogurt. Season to taste with salt and pepper. Pour the dressing over the salad and toss well. Serve with meat or fish.

Onion and Avocado Salad

4 slices bacon
½ avocado, peeled
  and sliced
2 teaspoons lemon
  juice
3 lettuce leaves,
  shredded
2 scallions, chopped
¼ cup salted peanuts
2 tablespoons French
  dressing (see page
  73)
salt and pepper

Cook the bacon in a skillet until crisp. Drain on paper towels and crumble.

Place the avocado slices in a serving bowl and sprinkle with the lemon juice. Add the lettuce, scallions, bacon, peanuts and French dressing. Toss well and season to taste with salt and pepper. Chill before serving.

Fruit Coleslaw

1 red apple, cored
  and chopped
2 teaspoons lemon
  juice
1 cup shredded
  cabbage
1 small carrot, grated
¼ cup chopped
  pitted dates
1 tablespoon raisins
10 seedless grapes,
  halved
2 tablespoons plain
  yogurt
2 tablespoons
  mayonnaise (see
  page 73)
salt and pepper

Place the apple in a bowl, sprinkle
with the lemon juice and toss well.
Add the cabbage, carrot, dates,
raisins and grapes.

Combine the yogurt, mayonnaise
and salt and pepper to taste. Pour the
dressing over the salad and toss well.
Spoon into serving bowls.

Cheese-Filled Avocado

1 avocado
1 teaspoon lemon
  juice
½ cup crumbled blue
  cheese
2 tablespoons small
  curd cottage cheese
salt and pepper
parsley sprigs for
  garnish

Halve the avocado, remove the pit and scoop out some of the flesh, leaving ½ inch thick shells. Reserve.

Place the avocado flesh and lemon juice in a bowl and mash with a fork. Blend in the cheeses and salt and pepper to taste.

Spoon the mixture into the avocado shells. Serve chilled, garnished with parsley.

Bean and Pasta Salad

1½ cups pasta shells
salt and pepper
½ cup canned red
   kidney beans,
   drained
½ green pepper,
   seeded and chopped
2 teaspoons chopped
   parsley
grated rind and juice
   of ½ orange
2 tablespoons French
   dressing (see page
   73)

Cook the pasta in plenty of boiling salted water until *al dente* (tender but still firm to the bite). Drain and rinse under cold running water.

Place the pasta in a serving bowl. Add the kidney beans, green pepper, parsley and orange rind. Mix the orange juice with the French dressing and add salt and pepper to taste. Pour the dressing over the salad and toss well. Chill before serving.

Creamy Potato Salad

½ lb new potatoes,
    cooked and chopped
few watercress sprigs,
    chopped
¼ cup chopped
    cooked ham
¼ cup heavy cream
1 teaspoon prepared
    mustard
pinch of sugar
salt and pepper
watercress sprigs for
    garnish

Place the potatoes (preferably while
still warm) in a bowl and add the
chopped watercress and ham.

Lightly whip the cream with the
mustard, sugar and salt and pepper
to taste. Add to the potatoes and mix
well.

Spoon into a serving dish.
Refrigerate for at least 30 minutes
before serving.

Garnish with watercress and serve
with cold cuts.

Apple and Nut Salad

2 apples, cored and
    chopped
2 teaspoons lemon
    juice
2 stalks celery,
    chopped
¼ cup salted peanuts
¼ cup chopped
    walnuts
3 tablespoons
    mayonnaise (see
    below)
few lettuce leaves
paprika

Place the apples in a bowl, sprinkle with lemon juice and toss well. Add the remaining ingredients, except the lettuce and paprika. Mix well.

Line two serving dishes with lettuce leaves and spoon the salad on top. Sprinkle with paprika.

French Dressing

1 tablespoon Dijon-
    style mustard
½ teaspoon sugar
1 teaspoon each
    finely chopped
    chives and parsley
5 tablespoons vinegar
10 tablespoons olive
    oil
salt and pepper

Combine the mustard, sugar and herbs. Stir in the vinegar. Pour into a screw-top jar and add the oil and salt and pepper to taste. Shake vigorously to blend before serving.
Makes about 1¼ cups

Mayonnaise

2 egg yolks
½ teaspoon salt
½ teaspoon pepper
½ teaspoon dry
    mustard
1 teaspoon sugar
1¼ cups olive oil
1½ tablespoons
    white vinegar or
    lemon juice

Make sure that all the ingredients are at room temperature.

Beat the egg yolks in a bowl with the salt, pepper, mustard and sugar. Add the oil, drop by drop, beating constantly. As the mayonnaise thickens the oil may be added in a thin stream.

When all of the oil has been added, gradually add the vinegar and mix thoroughly.
Makes about 1¼ cups

Raspberry Soufflé Omelet

¼ cup frozen
  raspberries,
  thawed and
  mashed
4 eggs, separated
2 tablespoons sugar
2 tablespoons water
pinch of salt
TO FINISH:
few whole raspberries
confectioners sugar

Place the raspberries in a greased shallow baking dish.

Beat the egg yolks and sugar together until pale. Stir in the water.

Beat the egg whites with the salt until stiff, then fold into the egg yolks. Pour over the raspberries and bake in a preheated 350°F oven for 15 to 20 minutes.

Top with the whole raspberries and sprinkle with confectioners sugar. Serve immediately with heavy cream.

Hazelnut Brûlée

½ lb seedless grapes
  or gooseberries
¼ cup sugar
¾ cup plain yogurt
¼ cup finely
  chopped hazelnuts
1 tablespoon brown
  sugar

Place the grapes in a saucepan with the sugar. Cover and simmer gently until the grapes are tender.

Spoon the grapes into individual ramekins and let cool. Combine the yogurt and hazelnuts and spoon on top of the grapes. Refrigerate.

Just before serving, sprinkle with the brown sugar and cook under a preheated broiler for 1 to 2 minutes or until the sugar has melted. Serve immediately.

Baked Bananas

2 bananas, thickly
  sliced
2 teaspoons lemon
  juice
1/4 cup chopped pitted
  dates
2 teaspoons honey
1 tablespoon water
1-2 tablespoons
  chopped walnuts

Place the bananas in a small baking
dish, add the lemon juice and toss
well. Sprinkle with the dates.

Combine the honey and water and
spoon over the bananas. Sprinkle
with the walnuts. Cover with foil
and bake in a preheated 350°F oven
for 20 minutes. Serve hot, with
heavy cream.

Date and Lemon Pudding

3 slices wholewheat
  bread, crusts
  removed, buttered
  and quartered
1/3 cup chopped pitted
  dates
1 egg
2 tablespoons brown
  sugar
1 teaspoon finely
  grated lemon rind
1/4 teaspoon ground
  allspice
1 1/4 cups milk

Arrange the bread in a greased
baking dish. Sprinkle with the dates.

Beat together the egg, 1
tablespoon of the sugar, the lemon
rind and allspice. Heat the milk, but
do not boil; stir into the egg mixture.

Pour the custard over the bread
and let stand for 10 to 15 minutes.
Place the dish in a roasting pan
containing enough water to come
halfway up the sides of the dish.
Bake in a preheated 350°F oven for
25 to 30 minutes or until the custard
is just set.

Sprinkle with the remaining sugar
and serve immediately.

Spiced Apple Amber

2 large tart apples,
  peeled, cored and
  sliced
1 tablespoon honey
1/4 teaspoon ground
  cinnamon
1/4 teaspoon grated
  nutmeg
1 tablespoon water
2 eggs, separated
1/4 cup sugar

Place the apples, honey, cinnamon,
nutmeg and water in a saucepan.
Heat gently until the apples are
tender. Cool slightly, then purée in a
blender or food processor. Beat in
the egg yolks, then spoon into a
small buttered baking dish.

Beat the egg whites until stiff, then
beat in half the sugar. Fold in the
remaining sugar and spoon the
meringue over the apples.

Bake in a preheated 350°F oven for
10 to 12 minutes. Serve hot.

Banana Splits with Fudge Sauce

2 bananas
4 small scoops
  vanilla ice cream
¼ cup heavy cream,
  whipped
2 teaspoons chopped
  nuts
2 glacé cherries
SAUCE:
1 square (1 oz)
  semi-sweet
  chocolate
1 tablespoon warm
  water
¼ cup firmly packed
  brown sugar
1 teaspoon corn
  syrup
⅛ teaspoon vanilla

Cut the bananas in half lengthwise. Place on individual serving dishes. Top each banana with two scoops of ice cream. Spoon or pipe the whipped cream on top and decorate with the nuts and cherries.

To make the sauce, melt the chocolate with the water in a heavy saucepan. Add the brown sugar and corn syrup. Heat gently, stirring, until the sugar has dissolved. Bring to a boil and boil steadily, without stirring, for 3 to 4 minutes. Remove from the heat and stir in the vanilla.

Pour the sauce over the banana splits or serve separately.

Spicy Orange Creamed Rice

3 tablespoons rice
1¼ cups milk
·¼ cup firmly packed
  brown sugar
1 teaspoon finely
  grated orange rind
¼ teaspoon grated
  nutmeg
2 tablespoons raisins
1 tablespoon butter or
  margarine

Place the rice in a baking dish. Add the remaining ingredients and stir well.

Bake in a preheated 325°F oven for 1½ to 2 hours, stirring twice during the first hour. Serve hot or cold.

Plum Tart

1 cup all-purpose
  flour
pinch of salt
1 teaspoon sugar
6 tablespoons butter
  or margarine
1 egg, beaten
FILLING:
¾ lb red plums,
  halved and pitted
⅔ cup water
¼ cup sugar
2 teaspoons
  cornstarch
confectioners sugar

Sift the flour and salt into a bowl and add the sugar. Cut in the butter until the mixture resembles fine bread crumbs. Add the egg and mix to a smooth dough. Knead lightly, cover and chill for 30 minutes.

Roll out the dough on a floured surface and use to line a 7 inch flan ring placed on a cookie sheet. Reserve the dough trimmings.

Place the plums, water and sugar in a saucepan. Cook gently until tender. Drain, reserving the juice.

Blend the cornstarch with the reserved juice in a saucepan. Bring to a boil, stirring. Add the plums and spoon into the pastry shell. Cut strips from the dough trimmings and make a lattice pattern over the plums.

Bake in a preheated 400°F oven for 25 minutes. Cool.

When cold, transfer the tart to a serving plate and sprinkle with confectioners sugar.

2 to 3 servings

Banana Orange Caramel

1 banana, sliced
1 pear, peeled, cored
    and sliced
pinch of ground
    cinnamon
grated rind and juice
    of ½ orange
1 tablespoon water
2 tablespoons sugar
2 eggs, beaten
toasted sliced almonds
    to decorate

Place the banana, pear, cinnamon and orange rind and juice in a saucepan and simmer for 5 minutes. Remove from the heat and let cool.

Place the water and sugar in a saucepan and heat gently until dissolved. Bring to a boil and boil steadily until a rich golden brown caramel is formed. Pour into buttered dariole molds or individual dishes.

Pour the eggs over the fruit mixture and stir well. Pour into the molds.

Place in a roasting pan containing enough water to come halfway up the sides of the molds. Bake in a preheated 300°F oven for 25 to 30 minutes or until just firm.

Chill in the refrigerator overnight. Just before serving, invert onto dishes and sprinkle with almonds. Serve with heavy cream.

Chocolate and Orange Mousse

2 squares (1 oz each)
  semi-sweet
  chocolate
2 tablespoons butter
  or margarine
grated rind and juice
  of ½ orange
1 egg, separated
¼ cup heavy cream,
  whipped
chocolate curls to
  decorate (see note)

Melt the chocolate in a bowl over a pan of hot water. Remove from the heat and add the butter, orange rind and juice and egg yolk. Beat until smooth. Let cool.

Fold in the whipped cream. Beat the egg white until stiff and fold into the chocolate mixture. Pour into individual dishes. Chill until set.

Decorate with chocolate curls before serving.

NOTE: To make chocolate curls, shave slivers from a bar of chocolate, using a potato peeler.

Ginger and Nut Ice Cream

¾ cup heavy cream
1 tablespoon milk
2 tablespoons
   confectioners sugar
3 tablespoons finely
   chopped stem
   ginger
2 teaspoons ginger
   syrup
2 tablespoons finely
   chopped hazelnuts

Place the cream and milk in a bowl and whip. Fold in the confectioners sugar. Pour into an ice cube tray, cover with foil and freeze for about 45 minutes or until ice crystals have formed around the sides of the tray.

Spoon into a chilled bowl and beat until smooth. Stir in the ginger, syrup and hazelnuts.

Pour into the ice cube tray, cover and freeze until firm.

Place in the refrigerator about 20 minutes before serving to soften. Spoon into individual dishes. Serve with cookies if desired.

Melon and Orange with Mint

½ honeydew melon
1 orange
few mint leaves,
   crushed
mint sprigs to
   decorate

Remove the seeds from the melon,
scoop out the flesh and chop into
pieces. Place in a bowl.

Grate the rind from the orange and
add to the melon. Peel and segment
the orange, discarding all the pith.
Add to the melon with the crushed
mint. Mix well and spoon into
individual serving dishes. Chill
before serving.

Decorate with mint sprigs and
serve with heavy cream.

Crunchy Apples

2 large apples,
  peeled, cored and
  sliced
2 tablespoons
  granulated sugar
1 teaspoon lemon
  juice
1 tablespoon water
¼ teaspoon ground
  cinnamon
2 tablespoons butter
  or margarine
¼ cup oatmeal
1 tablespoon brown
  sugar
¼ cup heavy cream
1 tablespoon milk
grated chocolate to
  decorate

Place the apples in a saucepan with
the granulated sugar, lemon juice,
water and cinnamon. Cook gently
until the fruit is soft. Mash until
smooth, then spoon into individual
glass serving dishes.

Melt the butter in a saucepan and
add the oatmeal and brown sugar.
Cook gently, stirring, until the
oatmeal is browned. Cool, then
spoon over the apples.

Whip the cream and milk together
lightly and spoon on top. Sprinkle
with grated chocolate.

Apricot and Chocolate Dessert

2 slices creme-filled
  chocolate jelly roll
4 canned apricot
  halves
¼ cup apricot yogurt
¼ cup heavy cream,
  whipped
grated chocolate to
  decorate

Place the cake in individual serving dishes. Drain the apricots and use a little of the syrup to moisten the cake. Chop the apricots and scatter over the cake.

Fold the yogurt into the whipped cream and spoon over the apricots. Sprinkle with grated chocolate. Serve chilled.

Blueberry Syllabub

1 cup blueberries
1/3 cup sugar
grated rind and juice
  of 1/2 lemon
2 tablespoons sherry
1/2 cup heavy cream

Place the blueberries, half of the sugar and the lemon rind and juice in a saucepan and cook gently for 5 minutes. Cool slightly, then process in a blender or food processor. Stir in the sherry.

Place the heavy cream, remaining sugar and half the blueberry purée in a bowl and beat until the mixture forms soft peaks.

Spoon the remaining blueberry purée into the bottom of two glasses and top with the whipped cream mixture. Chill before serving.

NOTE: Strawberries may be used instead of blueberries.

Pineapple Freeze

½ fresh pineapple
2 tablespoons water
½ cup confectioners
  sugar
mint sprigs to
  decorate

Cut the fruit from the pineapple,
discarding the core; reserve the shell.
Chop the fruit, place in a blender or
food processor with the water and
process until smooth. Stir in the
confectioners sugar.

Spoon the mixture into the reserved
shell, cover and freeze until firm.

Place in the refrigerator 20 minutes
before serving to soften. Decorate
with mint sprigs.

Apricot and Banana Cream

⅓ cup dried apricots
2 ripe bananas,
    chopped
1 teaspoon lemon
    juice
5 tablespoons heavy
    cream
2 tablespoons plain
    yogurt
2 teaspoons honey
walnut halves to
    decorate

Place the apricots in a bowl and add enough cold water to cover. Let soak for a few hours; drain well.

Place the bananas in a blender or food processor with the apricots, lemon juice, heavy cream, yogurt and honey. Process until smooth.

Spoon into individual glass serving dishes and chill before serving. Decorate with walnut halves.

Coffee Junket

1¼ cups milk
2 teaspoons sugar
1 teaspoon instant
    coffee
1 teaspoon essence of
    rennet
walnut halves to
    decorate

Place the milk, sugar and coffee in a saucepan. Heat gently, stirring to dissolve the coffee and sugar, until the mixture reaches 98°F or lukewarm.

Stir in the rennet and pour into individual serving bowls. Let stand at room temperature for 1½ hours or until set.

Chill before serving. Decorate with walnut halves.

Quick Rhubarb Fool

½ lb rhubarb,
    chopped
1 tablespoon water
grated rind of
    ½ orange
¼ cup sugar
½ cup heavy cream,
    whipped
¼ cup raspberry
    yogurt

Place the rhubarb in a saucepan with the water, orange rind and sugar. Cook gently until soft. Let cool, then process in a blender or food processor.

Fold two-thirds of the whipped cream into the rhubarb with the yogurt. Spoon into individual glass dishes and pipe swirls of whipped cream on top. Chill before serving.

Orange Cheesecake

2 tablespoons butter
    or margarine
1 cup graham cracker
    crumbs
FILLING:
1 cup small curd
    cottage cheese
2 tablespoons sugar
grated rind and juice
    of ½ orange
½ cup heavy cream,
    whipped
mandarin oranges to
    decorate

Melt the butter and stir in the crumbs. Press the mixture into the bottom and sides of a 7 inch quiche or flan dish. Chill in the refrigerator until firm.

Mix the cottage cheese with the sugar and orange rind and juice. Fold in the whipped cream. Spoon the mixture into the crumb crust.

Decorate with mandarin oranges. Chill before serving.
2 to 3 servings

Summer Fruits and Sour Cream Dessert

2 tablespoons sugar
1/4 cup water
1/2 lb red plums, pitted
3/4 cup raspberries
1/4 cup sour cream
2 teaspoons brown sugar

Place the sugar and water in a saucepan and heat gently until dissolved. Increase the heat and boil steadily for 2 minutes. Allow to cool, then chill.

Cut the plums into slices. Divide the plums and raspberries between individual serving dishes and pour the syrup over.

Spoon the sour cream over the fruit and sprinkle with brown sugar. Serve chilled.

Apple and Pear Ginger Trifle

1 apple, peeled,
  cored and sliced
1 pear, peeled, cored
  and sliced
1/4 cup apple cider
1/4 cup firmly packed
  brown sugar
1/4 teaspoon ground
  ginger
3 slices gingerbread,
  halved
1/2 cup heavy cream
1 tablespoon
  confectioners sugar
1 tablespoon chopped
  nuts

Place the apple and pear in a
saucepan with the apple cider, brown
sugar and ginger. Cook gently until
the fruit is just tender. Let cool.

Arrange the gingerbread in
individual glass serving dishes and
spoon the fruit and cooking liquid
over the top.

Lightly whip the cream and fold in
the confectioners sugar. Spoon over
the fruit and sprinkle with the nuts.
Serve chilled.

INDEX